Rev. Dr. J. P. Olarewaju

THE FRUITS OF
LIFE

Copyright © 2011 by Rev. John Peter Olarewaju. 102676-JOHN

ISBN: Softcover   978-1-4653-8102-6

All rights reserved. No part of this book may be reproduced or transmitted in any form or by any means, electronic or mechanical, including photocopying, recording, or by any information storage and retrieval system, without permission
in writing from the copyright owner.

To order additional copies of this book, contact:
Xlibris Corporation
1-888-795-4274
www.Xlibris.com
Orders@Xlibris.com

Table of Contents

FORWARD 4
INTRODUCTION 5
FRUIT 9
GO GREEN 13
GO NATURAL 14
EIGHT QUESTIONS & ANSWERS ABOUT DRINKING, DRUGS, SMOKING AND DRIVING. 15
STUDENTS 21
HIV 22
TIPS FOR HEALTHY LIVING 25
PREGNANT WOMAN 25
MAN 25
WOMAN 25
ELDERLY PEOPLE 25
OBESITY 25
LIVER 26
HAND WASHING 26
PETS 27
PEST 28

Forward

I thank the trinity, the father, the son and the Holy Ghost that gave me the wisdom, knowledge and understanding at authorship of books, teaching and evangelism. I also give thanks to the father almighty for making my dream about this book come to reality. This book will improve your diet and give you a better chance of living a healthy lifestyle. This book is published to save the lives in our world, of people that are suffering from illnesses through their consumption of fatty foods, and bring them to the Garden of Eden, to know the value of green vegetables and fruits to their health. This book will help a lot of lives that are in danger from HIV, drugs, and smoking. It is designed to change the lives of students and youth in our world. Also to delight the life of drivers and tell them the right thing to do to save the lives of passengers or their families that will travel with them. I also use this opportunity to thank my children, my wife and a lot of people in my church that their names are too numerous to mention in this book, especially my church committees in Toronto that made the dream of this book come to reality.

Introduction

There are different interpretations about the fruits of life. There is Fruit of life interpreted to be the word of God, and the other interpretation to be the fruits given to us as food from God. This book brings us back to the Garden of Eden, to remind us of the beginning of the world and teaches us about having good health through healthy foods. The scripture tells us in Genesis 1 vs.1 to the end, God created all the living creatures, fruits, leaves, trees and green herbs, and created Adam in his own image to have dominion over it.

Genesis 1 vs. 29 to 30:
²⁹God said, Behold, I have given you every herb bearing seed, which is upon the face of all the earth, and every tree, in the which is the fruit of a tree yielding seed; to you it shall be for meat. ³⁰And to every beast of the earth, and to every fowl of the air, and to every thing that creepeth upon the earth, wherein there is life, I have given every green herb for meat: and it was so.

My spiritual understanding tells me about disobedience to the word of God; to everyone that is born again in Christ without following what this scripture says, it is disobedience to the Lord and it could cause unhealthy life style. These verses further explain to us how dangerous it is to our health if we disobey the voice of the Lord by eating foods we call "delicious food". Of course, it may be delicious in taste, but it is unhelpful for your health. When we are talking about blessing, it is very difficult for some Christians to believe that blessing is not based on money alone; there are different types of blessing which we must ask from God. One of it is the blessing of good health that is, your good health comes from your balance diet and prayer. Truly, God created everything, both good and bad. But I advise you to eat the good ones and that is what God said through Moses his servant in

Deuteronomy 30:15
See, I have set before thee this day life and good, and death and evil
Proverb 30 vs. 8
⁸Remove far from me vanity and lies: give me neither poverty nor riches; feed me with food convenient for me.

Emphases the importance of natural fruits for a healthy life. Do you know how many years Adam lived in the Garden of Eden, before God created a helper for him?

<u>Geneses 2 vs.18-24</u>
¹⁸And the LORD God said, It is not good that the man should be alone; I will make him an help meet for him. ¹⁹And out of the ground the LORD God formed every beast of the field, and every fowl of the air; and brought them unto Adam to see what he would call them: and whatsoever Adam called every living creature that was the name thereof. ²⁰And Adam gave names to all cattle and to the fowl of the air and to every beast of the field; but for Adam there was not found an help meet for him. ²¹And the LORD God caused a deep sleep to fall upon Adam, and he slept: and he took one of his ribs, and closed up the flesh instead thereof; ²²And the rib, which the LORD God had taken from man, made he a woman, and brought her unto the man. ²³And Adam said, This is now bone of my bones, and flesh of my flesh: she shall be called Woman, because she was taken out of Man. ²⁴Therefore shall a man leave his father and his mother, and shall cleave unto his wife, and they shall be one flesh. 25And they were both naked, the man and his wife, and were not ashamed.

Throughout the years Adam lived in the garden, there were no hospitals, no doctors, no emergency attendants, and there is no day God visited him on the sick bed, because the scriptures tells us that God visited Adam every evening. Adam obeyed the instructions of God and lived in good health before he was betrayed by his wife (Eve) through Satan (serpent). All the life time of Adam in the Garden of Eden, before he disobeyed God, he didn't smoke, or taste alcohol, nor prepare any delicious food, other than the fruits and green vegetables provided for him by God in the garden. I advise all my readers to bring their life back to the Garden of Eden Spiritually and give up smoking, use of drugs, alcohol, and beware of the fatty foods you consume. Bring your daily meal to 75 per cent of fruit and vegetables. The bible tells us that, the Israelites were in the wilderness for 40 years without being sick, and they were always rejoicing with delicious food called **Manna**.

<u>Exodus 16 vs.10-19 & 35</u>
¹⁰And it came to pass, as Aaron spake unto the whole congregation of the children of Israel, that they looked toward the wilderness, and, behold, the glory of the LORD appeared in the cloud. ¹¹And the LORD spake unto Moses, saying, ¹²I have heard the murmurings of the children of Israel: speak unto them, saying, At even ye shall eat flesh, and in the morning ye shall be filled with bread; and ye shall know that I am the LORD your God. ¹³And it came to pass, that at even the quails came up, and covered the camp: and in the morning the dew lay round about the host. ¹⁴And when the dew that lay was gone up, behold, upon the face of the wilderness there lay a small round thing, as small as the hoar frost on the ground. ¹⁵And when the children of Israel saw it, they said one to another, It is manna: for they wist not what it was. And Moses said

unto them, This is the bread which the LORD hath given you to eat. ¹⁶This is the thing which the LORD hath commanded, Gather of it every man according to his eating, an omer for every man, according to the number of your persons; take ye every man for them which are in his tents. ¹⁷And the children of Israel did so, and gathered, some more, some less. ¹⁸And when they did mete it with an omer, he that gathered much had nothing over, and he that gathered little had no lack; they gathered every man according to his eating. ¹⁹And Moses said, Let no man leave of it till the morning. ³⁵And the children of Israel did eat manna forty years, until they came to a land inhabited; they did eat manna, until they came unto the borders of the land of Canaan.

It is written in the scripture, that God had roasted delicious quails for the children of Israel in the wilderness. They were satisfied with good health; they only got sick and die whenever they sinned against the Lord. Friends and readers, why can't you think about all this, and help your health, to keep away from smoking, drinking, and drug addiction and develop a love to eat fruits and green vegetables more often than the heavy traditional foods, because the Garden of Eden was created before our country, and the fruits were created before your traditional food. So, fruits are better than food, and fruits will make your health rejoice and you will live long with good health. You will have the opportunity to proclaim the liberty of God. Also your children will not regret in future about their blood inheritance from you. What can help you now is to pray to God to send down his comforter (The Holy Ghost) to your life. You may love those delicious fruits listed in this book to replace the love you have for traditional food, smoking, drugs or alcohol. Due to my spiritual knowledge, 65 per cent of teenagers that are smoking, and are addicted to drugs and alcohol on the street today, inherit it from their parents. 65 percent of murderers that are in prison or sentenced inherit the arrogant behaviours through their parents, and they increase their own evil character before they become murderers, smokers, drug addicts and alcoholics. Friends and readers, your health is very important for God. He loves you; he created you in his own image and made you the head, and the commander of all his creations,

<u>Genesis 1vs 26 & 27</u>
²⁶And God said, Let us make man in our image, after our likeness: and let them have dominion over the fish of the sea, and over the fowl of the air, and over the cattle, and over all the earth, and over every creeping thing that creepeth upon the earth. ²⁷So God created man in his own image, in the image of God created he him; male and female created he them.

For example, a director of a company expects the manager to perform excellently in his duties. God is your director and you are His manager. He expects you to be in good health and to perform excellently in His work in your life time. Not to train the nations how to smoke, not to train the nations about drug abuse, alcoholism or secret cultism.

Let me remind you what he said in the book of Psalm

<u>Psalm 19 vs 1</u>
The heavens declare the glory of God; and firmament sheweth his hand work.

Let us take a look at this verse. When God blessed the heaven that has no life, to declare his own glory, how much more you that He created in His own image. He expects us to declare His own glory more than the heaven, or the firmament to show His handwork. This is the reason why He needs your good health. This is the reason why I bring you back to the Garden of Eden, to be addicted to fruits and vegetables not to drugs, alcohol or smoking. I could remember when I was a teenager before I become a born-again Christian; I always drink a bottle of beer every night before I go to bed. My minimum cigarette in a day is 21 sticks. I would rather lend you one of my two pair shoes than give you a stick of cigarette, because I am not happy if I don't complete my 21 sticks daily. Allow me to share with you the experience I went through, I noticed continuous headache, which I always use pain killers to treat more than 3 or 4 times in a day. This caused problem of high blood pressure in my life before I was cured when I became a born-again Christian.
God has given us vegetables to make our hearts rejoice. Why are you then still relying on cigarette before you can be happy? Or the taking of drugs and alcohol before you can cheer up?

Fruit

Fruits and vegetables are healthy but not in the life of smokers, alcoholics and drug addicts. All the description and the usefulness of all ingredients in this book cannot work properly in your health until you quit smoking, taking of alcohol and drugs:
Let us see what Saint Paul explains to us in the book of Romans.

Romans 6v1 – end
Take a look at the life of the smokers in **vs 1**: *What shall we say then? Shall we continue in sin, that grace may abound?*

This means that smoking is one of the major sins. There is no grace of blessing of good health from God for Christians that are still in the sin of smoking or drinking; they are living in danger and risk of their lives. Let us look at **vs. 6**: *Knowing this, that our old man is crucified with him, that the body of sin might be destroyed, that henceforth we should not serve sin.*

Immediately you are baptized and born again the old spirit, I mean, the former behavior must be cast out from you, and you will receive the spirit of conscience. It is until you receive the spirit of conscience before you begin to realize your mistakes, and without realizing your mistakes you can not know that smoking, alcoholism and drug addiction are bad for your health. **vs.21**: *What fruit had ye then in those things whereof ye are now ashamed? for the end of those things is death.* Imagine if the use of illisit drug is good why then is it being hidden; we can eat fruit in the public and also food in the midst of friends. But anything you are feeling ashamed or afraid of doing in the open, is bad, for your peace of mind and health. It is evil in the sight of your family, and the law of all nations are against it.

Vs 22 & 23 tells us about everlasting life, what is everlasting life Everlasting? Everlasting life means good health and eternal life, and it cannot be found without being holy. God loves you, created you in his own image and he expects you to declare His glory in our world. Life is flexible, life is more delicate than you think. And without good health you cannot declare His glory properly.

²²But now being made free from sin, and become servants to God, ye have your fruit unto holiness, and the end everlasting life. ²³For the wages of sin is death; but the gift of God is eternal life through Jesus Christ our Lord.

Physiologically, the thought of alcoholics cannot imagine anything righteous, their hearts will always be full of evil thoughts and they can not forgive but the holiness of a man, comes from supernatural fruits from God, and their desire will be righteous.

<u>Ephesians 5:9</u>*: For the fruit of the Spirit is in all goodness and righteousness and truth;*

On my journey back from Ohio U.S.A to Toronto Canada in October 2006, I had a stop over in North Carolina almost three hours before joining my next flight to Toronto. There I met a man at a Christian bookshop in the airport, after we bought some books, we began discussing, he asked me two questions; he said, Reverend John, why do a lot of youths die nowadays And I said, Pastor Joseph, can you believe that all youths are walking out from the Garden of Aden, especially with what they are eating, and they don't allow the Holy Spirit to work in their lives. He then asked me again that why God created something good and bad together. There I took out my computer Bible in my hand luggage. I opened my Bible to
<u>**Deuteronomy 30:19, Genesis 1:29 and Genesis 3:3**</u>

<u>**Deuteronomy 30:19**</u> **I call heaven and earth to record this day against you, that I have set before you life and death, blessing and cursing: therefore choose life, that both thou and thy seed may live**

<u>Genesis 1:29</u>
And God said, Behold, I have given you every herb bearing seed, which is upon the face of all the earth, and every tree, in the which is the fruit of a tree yielding seed; to you it shall be for meat.

<u>Genesis 3:3</u>
But of the fruit of the tree which is in the midst of the garden, God hath said, Ye shall not eat of it, neither shall ye touch it, lest ye die.

After reading these Bible Chapters and verses, he agreed with me and there we ended the discussion then we departed. God warned Adam about the fruit he can eat and the fruit he must not touch but Adam disobeyed God through the Serpent and his wife and God was annoyed with him and disowned him. There he acknowledged death which he is supposed to live forever if he can obey the instruction and the commandment of God. This is the reason why I said until you come back to the Garden of Eden spiritually and obey the voice of God by not taking drugs, alcohol or smoking before you can live long with good health. You can imagine that someone can live for nine hundred years in the land of living without going through operation or sickness. People like Methuselah and Noah. Let us go to the book of **_Genesis_** It will enlighten you that there is possibility for you to live long with good health.

Genesis 5 vs. 1-end
This is the book of the generations of Adam. In the day that God created man, in the likeness of God made he him; ²Male and female created he them; and blessed them, and called their name Adam, in the day when they were created. ³And Adam lived an hundred and thirty years, and begat a son in his own likeness, after his image; and called his name Seth: ⁴And the days of Adam after he had begotten Seth were eight hundred years: and he begat sons and daughters: ⁵And all the days that _Adam_ lived were nine hundred and thirty years: and he died. (_930 years_) ⁶Seth lived an hundred and five years, and begat Enos: ⁷And Seth lived after he begat Enos eight hundred and seven years, and begat sons and daughters: ⁸And all the days of _Seth_ were nine hundred and twelve years: and he died. (_912 years_) ⁹Enos lived ninety years, and begat Cainan: ¹⁰And Enos lived after he begat Cainan eight hundred and fifteen years, and begat sons and daughters: ¹¹And all the days of _Enos_ were nine hundred and five years: and he died. (_905 years_) ¹²And Cainan lived seventy years, and begat Mahalaleel: ¹³And Cainan lived after he begat Mahalaleel eight hundred and forty years, and begat sons and daughters: ¹⁴And all the days of _Cainan_ were nine hundred and ten years: and he died (_910 years_). ¹⁵And Mahalaleel lived sixty and five years, and begat Jared: ¹⁶And Mahalaleel lived after he begat Jared eight hundred and thirty years, and begat sons and daughters: ¹⁷And all the days of _Mahalaleel_ were eight hundred ninety and five years: and he died. (_895 years_) ¹⁸And _Jared_ lived an hundred sixty and two years, and he begat Enoch: ¹⁹And Jared lived after he begat Enoch eight hundred years, and begat sons and daughters: ²⁰And all the days of _Jared_ were nine hundred sixty and two years: and he died. (_962 years_). ²¹Enoch lived sixty and five years, and begat Methuselah: ²²And Enoch walked with God after he begat Methuselah three hundred years, and begat sons and daughters: ²³And all the days of Enoch were three hundred sixty and five years: ²⁴And _Enoch_ walked with God: and he was not; for God took him. (_365 years_) ²⁵Methuselah lived an hundred eighty and seven years, and begat Lamech: ²⁶And Methuselah lived after he begat Lamech seven hundred eighty and two years, and begat sons and daughters: ²⁷And all the days of _Methuselah_ were nine hundred sixty and nine years: and he died (_969 years_). ²⁸And _Lamech_ lived an hundred eighty and two years, and begat a son: ²⁹And he called his name Noah, saying, this same shall comfort us concerning our work and toil of our hands, because of the ground which the LORD hath cursed. ³⁰And Lamech lived after he begat Noah five hundred ninety and five years, and begat sons and daughters: ³¹And all the days of _Lamech_ were seven hundred seventy and seven years: and he died (_777 years_).

<u>Genesis 9 vs. 28-29</u> ²⁸ Noah lived after the flood three hundred and fifty years. ²⁹And all the days of Noah were nine hundred and fifty years: and he died. (950 years)

Let us go little further with the story of Noah, which I believe that all the readers of this book will learn a lesson in his story. You need to realize that you've been blessed from birth. But due to the sinful ways some people follow concerning alcohol, it can delay the blessing till the end of your life. The end of a drunkard will be worse than the beginning thereof. The scripture tells us that Noah was blessed from God because of the good job he did in building the Ark and obeying the voice of the Lord for rescuing a lot of lives during the great flood. But at the end, he became an alcoholic and the Holy Ghost departed from him. He cursed his son with a grievous curse, "His own blood".

<u>Genesis 9 vs. 20-27</u>

²⁰And Noah began to be an husbandman, and he planted a vineyard: ²¹And he drank of the wine, and was drunken; and he was uncovered within his tent. ²²And Ham, the father of Canaan, saw the nakedness of his father, and told his two brethren without. ²³And Shem and Japheth took a garment, and laid it upon both their shoulders, and went backward, and covered the nakedness of their father; and their faces were backward, and they saw not their father's nakedness.

²⁴Noah awoke from his wine, and knew what his younger son had done unto him. ²⁵And he said, Cursed be Canaan; a servant of servants shall he be unto his brethren. ²⁶And he said, Blessed be the LORD God of Shem; and Canaan shall be his servant. ²⁷God shall enlarge Japheth, and he shall dwell in the tents of Shem; and Canaan shall be his servant.

God blessed Noah. He was a Ship captain, a leader and elder of all living creatures for months before the dry land. At the end of his live, he became a drunkard and destroys the life of his son. Can you imagine how dangerous alcohol is? Can you imagine what can happen to your future at the end of your alcoholism? Do you know the damages alcohol may bring to your health at the end of your life? I can tell you through the result of my research about alcohol. Alcoholics are a living dead. What I mean by that is that they die before their day, I advise you to quit drinking alcohol.

Go Green

What I mean by go green is returning to green vegetables, herbs, fruits, flowers and woods. Live in the midst of trees and flowers, especially if gardens can be planted surrounding your residence. For example, if you listen to the songs of birds, it is quite different and it shows the sign of happiness. People that have gardens surrounding there houses live healthy. Most of the oxygen we breathe in comes from trees and plants. So, by planting gardens around your homes, you'll get more fresh air. Trees give you fresh and supernatural oxygen and get rid of carbon dioxide that is the air you breathe out. Gardens beautify your houses. It is good to live in places that surrounded by trees and flowers, because when God created us, puts us in a garden: "The Garden of Eden". He did this so that we will not be sick and we can live long. But nowadays there are so many factories that pollute the air. So, when you are surrounded by trees, lakes and plants, you'll feel healthy and comfortable. That is why most farmers have good health and are strong. Another thing that makes farmers strong and healthy is because they eat fruits that come directly from the trees, rather than the force ripened ones common in our society.

Go Natural

Skin-disease

Anything natural provides you good health, long life, happiness and joy. Go natural, about your food, go natural about the way you live. For example, you must be careful about using a strong chemical to clean your carpet or pots. This can cause a critical illness. The strong soap that people used in bleaching their body also causes skin disease. Go natural and be careful of fried foods, they are high in cholesterol content. Go natural about cleaning your fruits and foods before eating it.

Exercise

Exercising is good for your health in a lot of ways. It fights against heart attack, obesity, headaches, small fevers and it also keeps you in shape. Exercising 3 times a week will surely keep you away from the doctors. It will make you feel strong and energetic. Exercising is good for people of all ages.

Drug addict , Smokers and Alcoholism

Drug addicts, smokers and drunkards live a dangerous and delicate life. Smoking or drinking is the natural progression to drugs addiction. Drug addiction may also lead to mental illness. If you are a drug addict, drunkard or smoker, it is not too late to quit. I know it's not easy to quit, flesh can not allow you but through the power of Holy Ghost and deliverance from any born again church, your life will change. The power of Satan through addiction is broken now in Jesus name. Some people say the way they live their lives is a personal issue that concerns nobody but themselves. But be informed that addictions does not only destroy your life, it also affects the lives of your family and friends. For instance, if ten thousand people bought good cars in your community, people will say that there is a lot of wealth in that society and will like to live in that area. Conversely, if there are ten thousand drugs addicts in your community, people will warn their children not to look for jobs in that area, because it is occupied with drug addicts. Before you realize it, your gangs will be up to thousands of people. Now you will understand that the drugs, smoking or alcohol, will destroy not only your life alone, but also the children and your community, and the whole country. I advise you to quit.

Eight Questions & Answers
ABOUT DRINKING, DRUGS, SMOKING AND DRIVING.

QUESTION NUMBER ONE:
Is it good to drink and drive?

The question can be answered in two senses, yes, no. A lot of people say yes, because alcohol makes them smart in driving, gives them power and doesn't make them to be afraid of the road. For example, some unexpected occasions may cause sharing a glass of alcohol together with a friend, do you expect us to leave our car there? This is why a lot of people say yes to drinking and driving. The correct answer is <u>NO</u>. Because drinking and driving cause fatal accident.

Alcohol gives you an over confidence mind when driving, and makes you over speed.
Eighty percent of accident that causes serious injuries and takes a lot of life happens under influence alcohol.

Alcohol makes you dizzy, feel sleepy and tired after it leaves your system. This may cause an accident, and this kind of accident may cost lives, because, either the vehicle leaves the road, flips and jumps over a bridge into a gully, or crash into another persons house along the road. We call this kind of incident a fatal accident and all these came through due to influence of alcohol.

QUESTION NUMBER TWO:
Is it good to smoke when driving?

The question can be answered in two senses, Yes, No. Some people say <u>YES</u>, because smoking on the steering makes them enjoy driving. It keeps them busy on the steering and makes them concentrate to what they are doing, and also gives them the joy of the journey.
But the correct answer is **<u>NO.</u>**
The reason why is that, your smoke from your cigarette cause damages to the health of your family / passengers inside your vehicle.
Another way that makes it dangerous, if another person in the vehicle is a smoker like you there is the likelihood of ashes being blown into the driver's eye thereby blinding him/her and causing an accident that may take lives or cause a lot of injuries.
I say no to smoking when driving because the nicotine may not work normal with your blood sometimes when you are hypertensive, this can cause over speeding and a serious accident. I said this because I was a smoker when I was a teenager. It may be the same cigarette, but you are not in the same mood all the time. Smoking when driving can make you dizzy due to the system of your blood at that hour. This can make you leave the road and go the wrong way, and we call this a stupid mistake. It may takes lives or causes serious injuries to your passengers or your family that are traveling with you.

QUESTION NUMBER THREE:
*Is it good to drive under the influence of **'DRUGS'**?*

There are also two ways to answer this question. Yes and No. From my findings a lot of people say yes, because it makes them smart not to be sluggish or get dizzy while diving. They said drugs give them patience against the violence of the passenger. It protects them against sickness and takes away the fear of the police and accident that can occur during their journey. But the absolute answer in **NO**. It is no because the advantages of drugs and driving is (0) zero percent. So the total answer is **NO**.

Drugs doesn't help your health. All your organs are in danger of sudden collapse if you are a drug addict, and I assure you that there is no drug addict that can live long. Drugs make you do everything abnormally, and the accident of a drug addict will be fatal. Drug is against the law of the government of all nation. If hard drug is good for you, why then is it hidden? And would be approved by the government law. Using hard drugs is tantamount to committing suicide because they drain you. To God, hard drug is a sin.

Do you know that the children produced by the blood of drug addicts cannot be normal or behave like normal children? The appearance, behaviors and dressing of drug addicts are different in a wrong way; a lot of people commit suicide because they don't know what they are doing after taking drugs. A lot people commit murder due to the drug addiction influence, and a lot of people run crazy because their blood is against it. The final conclusion is that drugs and driving is a NO, NO and a total NO. shelah

Is it good to drive after having a misunderstanding or arguments? The answer to this question is YES and NO.

A lot of people would say yes to this question because giving a little gap when an argument arises is very important in the life of a child of God. The solution to this matter is to take your car and leave the environment. But the correct answer is NO. It is a good idea if you can leave the environment and keep away for few hours to allow everyone involved in the argument to calm down. But do not drive because the Bible says in the book of:

<u>*James 1 vs. 20&21*</u>
[20]*For the wrath of man worketh not the righteousness of God.* [21]*Wherefore lay apart all filthiness and superfluity of naughtiness, and receive with meekness the engrafted word, which is able to save your souls.*
Let me tell you the real facts, the problem or the accident you are going to encounter on your way with anger will be more fatal than the problem you left at home. So the absolute answer is no. It is no because you may destroy the lives of innocent people through anger. So its better you join a public transport or walk away with your foot. As a matter of fact you do not need to walk away from all argument or misunderstanding. Bitterness of mind needs patience, prayer and comfort because; it affects your behaviors towards people you will meet on your way out. See what the bible says in the book of:

<u>*Job 21 vs. 25*</u>
[25]*And another dieth in the bitterness of his soul, and never eateth with pleasure.*

QUESTION NUMBER FOUR:

Is it good to answer your call when driving?

There are two possible answers to this question too. Yes and No. A lot of people argue yes, because they may be on the highway, where there's nowhere to park and an emergence call comes through from either family at home or boss at work. They say it is justifiable to pick it up calls and drive at the same time. Some say they have hands free device. And it is permanent in their ear while driving. Therefore, they are not disturbed in answering the calls when driving. But the correct answer is **NO**. Because the answering of your call either while you holding the phone or answering by hands free or through a phone speaker inside your vehicle is distracting. I want you to realize that any word that comes out of your mouth comes from your brain. Also your normal driving comes through the brain and two of them cannot work at full concentration together. Either you lose concentration on what you're saying on the phone, or in your driving. The brain cannot control these two things together. This is a cause of a lot of accidents. I personally has witnessed 3 or 4 accident like that, in different countries. Once again, the absolute answer is **NO**. The solution is to park and answer your call, or call the person back, when you arrive at a safe destination.

QUESTION NUMBER FIVE:

Is it good to drive yourself to the hospital when you get sick and there is no one around?

The question can be answered in two ways. Yes and No. Some people say yes, that is the right thing to do when someone is sick and is still fit to drive him or herself to the hospital when there is no one around to help. That's the best thing to do is to help themselves. But the correct answer is **NO**, because a lot of people die on the steering. You cannot predict what can happen to someone that is sick in few hours. The best thing to do in a situation like this is to call for help. Call the ambulance, friends or relatives and continue to pray till God sends you a helper.

QUESTION NUMBER SIX:

Is it good to disobey the police when they stop your car by run away? Yes or No.

Some people would say yes because they are afraid of the police. Hence, they like to run from police because the police cannot stop you without finding an offence in your car. Some give excuses about the problem that could happen if they stop for the police or respect them. But the answer is NO put it in mind to obey the laws of the government. As a matter of fact, the police are one of the most respected government workers. When we are talking about Canadian police, American police, German police, and also the English police, they are well respected officers, and follow the instruction of their government and protect their citizens. In most African countries on the contrary, governments take their policemen and women for granted, that is why a lot of people don't respect the police in other countries. My advice to everyone is to obey the police any time they pull you over. The police are your friends, they are your protector, they are there for you to tell you your rights as a citizen. Running from the police when they are being stopped you is a criminal offence. What can happen to you when you refuse to stop for the police will be very bad, it may be a fatal accident or something else. But my final advice is to obey the police anytime they pull you over.

QUESTION NUMBER SEVEN:

Is it good to drive at night to avoid traffic when traveling to a long distance? The answer is Yes or No.

Many people that are used to long distance driving would say yes to driving at night. They say yes because they want to avoid the aggressive drivers and a lot of cars that can cause delays and accidents. But the correct answer is **NO**. I say no because night driving is **DANGEROUS,** but not everywhere. For example, there is no problem in night driving in Canada, our roads are good, there is protection, and there are nothng like armed robbers, you may drivie all night without problem. But in other countries where there is no much protection, or good roads and there are problems of armed robbers and most of their cars are not strong enough, it is very dangerous to drive at night. So, the absolute answer is no, night drviving is very dangerous.

Let us talk about accident that may happen at night; this is a dangerous risk in countries where government ambulances are not provided, because accidents has no master, it can happen to anybody where there is nobody to rescue those that are hurt, this can take away lives. Let us talk about the breakdowns of the vehicles at night. What can you do when there is no one to rescue or help you when there are no night mechanics or towing vehicles? Think about this and know that night driving is dangerous. Finally, the answer is **NO**.

Students

This is an advice to all the students of the world. You should not help your education; let your education help your future. Be serious with your study and use your normal brain to complete your education. That is how the education will help you. The students that help their education by exam malpractices, who cannot read or sit for exams with a clear brain without drugs, smoking or drinking alcohol. This is why a lot of university graduates are jobless; they are jobless because they are drug addicts, smokers and alcoholics. Because no matter how they pretend; it will emanate at interviews and all their qualifications become useless. Some students get someone to write their exams their behalf. Surely they will have a qualified certificate but their brain is empty, and they will find it difficult to find a job. This can lead them to a dirty job or a bad gang. At the end of it they will become a smoker, drunkard or drug addict. Some students forget their education because of love. Love is the third step when you are in a higher education, the first step is to be serious with your study, and to know what you are doing. After graduation, the second step is to set up your business, or to look for a good job. The third step is love. Love, marriage and family are the main center of the life of a human being. But love doesn't allow some students to study. Remember that when things fall apart, the center holds no more. The meaning of this is that if you fail your final exam, you can't find a good job. As far as you can't find a good job, you cannot prepare for a happy family. Finally, students, you must be serious with the first step which is your education, and remember that you shouldn't help your education, but let your education help your future. Because, any certificate that you have or received by drugs may be useless in future, it will not work for you. To understand and to follow this instruction, you must be reading and pray very fervently, for wisdom, knowledge and understanding. And you must remember that you are the salt, light and the future of our world. God bless the readers and the author of this book. **AMEN.**

2ⁿᵈ Peter 1 vs. 5-10
⁵And beside this, giving all diligence, add to your faith virtue; and to virtue knowledge; ⁶And to knowledge temperance; and to temperance patience; and to patience godliness; ⁷And to godliness brotherly kindness; and to brotherly kindness charity. ⁸For if these things be in you, and abound, they make you that ye shall neither be barren nor unfruitful in the knowledge of our Lord Jesus Christ. ⁹But he that lacketh these things is blind, and cannot see afar off, and hath forgotten that he was purged from his old sins. ¹⁰Wherefore the rather, brethren, give diligence to make your calling and election sure: for if ye do these things, ye shall never fall:

HIV

HIV is a virus that doesn't have a cure presently. It kills and destroys families. HIV is not a disease, it is an angel from Heaven to judge the world.

<u>Revelation 16 vs. 1 to 12</u>
¹And I heard a great voice out of the temple saying to the seven angels, Go your ways, and pour out the vials of the wrath of God upon the earth. ²And the first went, and poured out his vial upon the earth; and there fell a noisome and grievous <u>sore</u> upon the men which had the mark of the beast and upon them which worshipped his image.

I want you to understand what verses one and two says about the poison the angel pour out to the world, and if you take notice about the sore the verse two mentioned, you will realize that it is the sign of the HIV virus.

³And the second angel poured out his vial upon the sea; and it became as the blood of a dead man: and every living soul died in the sea. ⁴And the third angel poured out his vial upon the rivers and fountains of waters; and they became blood. ⁵And I heard the angel of the waters say, Thou art righteous, O Lord, which art, and wast, and shalt be, because thou hast judged thus.

We have heard clearly what is written in verses three to seven, if care is not taken both the sea and ocean, and the lake will be dangerous in a few years to come, because the angel came to revenge the innocent souls and ministers of God that were killed. A lot of men today chase and sleep with other men's wives in the name of giving out jobs, money or help and the women also sleep around in the name of providing food for their family; this powerful people rule our world with power, they rule our world with personality and dishonor and without the fear of the lord. This angel that is called AIDS came to judge, especially the fornicators. It is a pity that there are not many righteous people in the world today that potends ill for most of the inhabitants of this world. <u>Unfortunately it is not only the sinners that will surfer, but some innocent souls will partake of this second death.</u> HIV is the second death, which means one dies while still alive.
⁸And the fourth angel poured out his vial upon the sun; and power was given unto him to scorch men with fire. ⁹And men were scorched with great heat, and blasphemed the name of God, which hath power over these plagues: and they repented not to give him glory. ¹⁰And the fifth angel poured out his vial upon the seat of

the beast; and his kingdom was full of darkness; and they gnawed their tongues for pain, [11]And blasphemed the God of heaven because of their pains and their sores, and repented not of their deeds. [12]And the sixth angel poured out his vial upon the great river Euphrates; and the water thereof was dried up, that the way of the kings of the east might be prepared.

Interpretations of verses eight to twelve in another way how this angel prophesied about the future of AIDS in our world. If care is not taken, it will become a virus that we can inhale through air and the sun like the SARS virus, and by then our animal, lakes, dams and bore holes will be very dangerous. But fear not you righteous, you will escape the second death

The word of God says that you righteous; are blessed and saved because you are walking in the holiness of the Lord. You are blessed and saved. Scientists discovered that HIV comes from Monkeys and Gorillas. But remember that there are gorillas thousands of years ago and we heard about this sickness. In the life of Noah, God destroyed this world with flood at that time and God said it will not happen again.

<u>Genesis 9vs 11</u>
[11]And I will establish my covenant with you; neither shall all flesh be cut off any more by the waters of a flood; neither shall there anymore be a flood to destroy the earth.

God destroyed Sodom and Gomorrah with fire and God doesn't want that to happen again.

<u>Genesis 19 vs 27-29</u>
[27]And Abraham gat up early in the morning to the place where he stood before the LORD: [28]And he looked toward Sodom and Gomorrah, and toward all the land of the plain, and beheld, and, lo, the smoke of the country went up as the smoke of a furnace. [29]And it came to pass, when God destroyed the cities of the plain, that God remembered Abraham, and sent Lot out of the midst of the overthrow, when he overthrew the cities in which Lot dwelt.

The angels of judgment is in our world to judge the sinners, especially the sexually immoral. The name of the angel is AIDS. Out of the judgment of sinners you righteous must be careful not to be judged, because husband may be righteous and the wife a sinner, or wife may be righteous and the husband a sinner. Therefore, you may contact it through sexual intercourse. Other ways by which this disease can be contacted are through nail cutter, or clipper, needles for those that use an already used needle to inject themselves. Also, the use of the same toothbrush by multiple users; because of ulcers and injuries in the mouth is very dangerous. Kissing is dangerous as well, kissing those that have wounds on their tongues or gums without knowing can cause infection. Blood transfusion is also dangerous if it comes from an HIV positive donor without knowing. We need to come together with cooperation and work seriously on HIV AIDS to find the cure, protection of our future generation, how to protect our air and water against it. I am saying the real facts spiritually, the six billion lives that are in our world today will hardly remain two billion in the year 2060, because a lot of pregnancy will be terminated through HIV positive of their parents and a lot of children will be carriers of the disease and die prematurely . What I mean is that the babies born every year are reducing and HIV AIDS victims are increasing. This will bring a lot of set backs to people living in our planet in fifty three years time. Beware of Hepatitis, Hepatitis A, B and C are HIV junior. You must clean your cups and spoons properly before use. Eating a lot of fruits will help you fight against HIV, HIV kills, beware of It.

Tips for Healthy Living

PREGNANT WOMAN

Blend some carrots with little mangoes and half an orange with one apple, drink it twice in a week; it will help your baby to be strong and protect the baby against any inheritance sicknesses.

MAN

Blend one apple with one carrot with little coconut and the coconut water, drink it once in a week and it will make you strong like a man.

WOMAN

It is easier for a woman to capture cancer, through the pregnancy protection pill. They can also contact breast cancer if the baby do not suck their milk for three to six months. To prevent this blend one apple and some grapes with half a banana, drink it two times in a week, it will protect you from breast cancer.

ELDERLY PEOPLE

Blend pear and green paw-paw with apple like juice for your elderly man or woman, twice every week; it will keep him/her away from the doctor. It will make them strong till the end of their life.

OBESITY

Small amount of Meat, fish, egg, cheese, milk, vegetable and wheat germ serves as protein. Build all the cells in your body with protein. Any lack of this nitrogenous substance affects the eyes detrimentally and brings a lot of fat to the body. This will cause over hyper ness and over hyper ness will make you feel hungry every hour before you realize this you will become over weighed. That is obesity.

LIVER

The functions of the liver are to store glycogen to produce bile to excrete waste product (E.G. URINE) Liver is one of the most respectful organs in your system. Without a good liver, there is no good health. It Makes it easier for your body to function. Many drinks and foods that you eat is probably not very good for your liver and kidney. Having a weak liver will make you feel uncomfortable. You must make sure that you eat healthy things such as beans and grapes to sustain your liver, and beware of too much salt, alcohol, too much maggi, anything colouring and you need a lot of water everyday to sustain your liver and maintain your kidney.

HAND WASHING

To protect your health against diseases, you must make sure you clean your hand before you taste anything. Because, different types of germs that we can not see without a microscope are hanged at the door knob and car doors that you touch in your daily journey. This is a serious warning for all the readers of this book that you must clean your hand very well before you touch anything you want to eat.

Pets

CATS

Cats are one of the most loved pets living together with human beings at home. But due to our research, you must be careful about what cats bite, not to taste it. Especially, the fur of cats are dangerous, this is why you must warn your children not to sleep with cats under the same quilt, or on the same bed as a lot of children normally love to do with their pets. Repercussion of this can result to tuberculosis or terrible asthma, or it can cause retaining coughs, the meaning of retaining cough is a standby cough that renews itself every year and no treatment can cure it. It may come at any time, and leave at any time, but comes every year.

DOGS

Dogs are good pets, they behave like human beings, and some trained dogs obey the voice of their master. According to the research about the blood of dogs. God gave dogs special blood cure that maintains their organs and protects their blood against germs, which we can not find in the blood of human beings. Because of this, you should be careful not to allow dogs to lick your open cuts or sores. There are dangerous bugs under the fur of dogs, it is a big risk and dangerous for your cuts or sores to be exposed to this bug. This is why lunatic sicknesses happens to a lot of old aged people. They may not remember their closeness with their dogs years ago, especially the kinds of cuddles they have with their dogs. Mind you, I am not condemning dogs. Dogs are good pets, but keep them at home like dogs and take care of them, not like a wife/ husband or children. In some villages in Africa where there are no veterinarians, you will realize that dogs will lick their open wounds until it closes up without treatment. Can't you realize that the tongues of dogs have special portions that are not the same like the human being's tongues. But you will be surprised that a lot of people kiss dogs, they may not realize it until years later, and this can bring skin cancer. Still they will not remember where they came across it, but their doctors might predict it transferred through blood transfusion or sexual intercourse or inheritance from their parents, without them knowing that this came from an animal years ago.

GOATS

In Africa, goats are pets in homes. But in Canada, goats lives on farms and farmers take proper care of them. Goats are clean animals with good meats. If you have a goat at home, be careful, because the mucus of goats is dangerous in your foods or fresh fruits. This could affect your liver or cause stomach sore called ulcer. Warning: do not be careless with your food or fruit anywhere there is a goat.

Pest

Lizard

Lizards are not common around world. The cold in western world does not allow them to live all round the year because lizards are mostly found in warm countries/continent such as Africa. People living in areas where lizards are common must be careful not to drink uncovered water. A lizard's tongue is poisonous. Drinking infected with a lizard's poison is dangerous. Same as eating foods, fruits or meat infected with a lizard's poison. It may affect your kidney years later and can cause continuous boils in any parts of your body. Also, it could cause skin disease such as rashes. Beware of lizards.

Cockroach

All cockroaches all over the world are look alike, but different attitudes. African cockroaches bite and suck human blood, also destroys clothes placed in a box. But Canadian cockroaches doesn't, and pest controls docsn't allow cockroaches to live in Canada. Therefore, eating food or fruits touched by cockroach are in risk of typhoid; typhoid may lead to liver problem and liver problems may also lead to Hepatitis A, B and C. It could cause yellow eyes and Hepatitis is dangerous like HIV. Warning: beware of cockroaches, don't let them live in your premises. They are dangerous.

Rats

Rats are not pest that you can allow to live in your premises, rats kill, transfer sicknesses, and poisoning from rat may affect your sight in old age.

Contents Of Fruits

The Fruits 31
APPLE 31
APRICOT 32
ARTICHOKES 32
AVOCADO/PEAR 33
BANANA 33
BEANS 33
BEETS 34
BITTER LEAF 34
BLUEBERRIES 34
BREAD 35
BROCCOLI 35
CABBAGE 36
CASSAVA 36
CASSAVA LEAVES 36
CASHEW 37
CANTALOUPE 37
CARROTS 37
CAULIFLOWER 38
CHERRIES 38
CHESTNUTS 39
COCOYAM 39
COCONUT 39
COCOA 40
COFFEE FRUIT 40
CORN 40
CRAB 41
CUCUMBER 41
EGGS 42
FIGS 42
FISH 42
FLAX 43
GARLIC 43
GINGER 43

GUAVA	44
GRAPEFRUIT & GRAPES	44
KIWI	45
LEMONS & LIMES	45
LETTUCE	46
MUSHROOM	46
OATS	47
OKRA	47
ONIONS	47
ORANGES & TANGERINE	48
PALM FRUIT	48
PAWPAW	49
PEACHES	50
PEAR	50
PEANUTS	50
PEPPERS	51
PINEAPPLE	51
PLANTAIN	52
PRUNES	52
POMEGRANATE	53
RICE	53
SHRIMPS	54
SOUR SOP	54
STRAWBERRIES	55
SNAIL	55
SWEET POTATOES	56
SUGAR CANE	56
SPINACH	57
TOMATOES	57
WALNUTS	58
WATER	58
WATERMELON	59
WHEAT GERM	59
WHEAT BRAN	60
YAM	60
The Word of Appreciation	61

The Fruits

Life is good health and what is health? Health is wholeness of the body, mind and spirit .Without good health there is no life. Food and prayer provide good health. Food and ungodliness may cause damages to your health. I advise you to rebuke greediness in your life, so you will be satisfied with any little food or fruit that you may have daily. Fruits and vegetables must be seventy five percent of your daily food; surely, this shall provide you with good health and long life. Finally, you are welcome to the life market and take a look at the wares and ingredients of good health.

APPLE

Joel 1:12:
The vine is dried up, and the fig tree languisheth; the pomegranate tree, the palm tree also, and the apple tree, even all the trees of the field, is withered: because joy is withered away from the sons of men.

Apple is one of the fruits that God recommends for your family, the book of Joel says that there is no joy in the life, health or family that lacks of it. Apple protects your heart against heart attack, cleans your kidney and makes your eyes clear, one apple a day keeps you away from the doctor. Apples are very good for a pregnant woman and it helps her baby also. You can eat fresh apples; you can cook it before eating. It is good for pie, which is very good for your health. Apple juice is very good for your health if you do not have diabetics.

APRICOT

Apricots are fruits of knowledge and eating it often will freshen your memory and make your eyes clear. Apricots will give you low cholesterol, it is one of nature best fruits you should eat it at least twice every week.

ARTICHOKES

Genesis 1:29
And God said, Behold, I have given you every herb bearing seed, which is upon the face of all the earth, and every tree, in the which is the fruit of a tree yielding seed; to you it shall be for meat.

ARTICHOKES are one of the herbs that God presents for your good health. Cooking it with rice or preparing it with stew to eat yam, plantain, cocoyam etc. May low your cholesterol, protects you from heart attacks, protect your liver and lowers your blood sugar

AVOCADO/PEAR

Avocadoes butter is supernatural. Eating your bread, plantain and yam with avocado's butter will lower your blood pressure. It will lower your cholesterol and make your skin smooth. Avocado's nut is iron eating it after cooking will help your health

BANANA

Proverbs 18:20
A man's belly shall be satisfied with the fruit of his mouth; and with the increase of his lips shall he be filled.

You do not need to be hungry before eating a banana. Bananas are fruits of refreshment. It is good to eat the yellow ones as it is or eat it with rice. You can cook the green bananas before eating it. Bananas are good for your heart and it make your bones strong, lowers your blood pressure and digest your food easily. Bananas are one of the supernatural foods for it is very good.

BEANS

Bean is protein. Eating it regularly will lower your cholesterol and your blood sugar. Beans wages war against cancer and provides more blood. Beans are a very good food.

BEETS

Beets are delicious fruit. It is good because it controls your blood pressure. Cooking the leaves with stew will help protect you from heart disease. Also eating the fruit regularly will make your bone strong.

BITTER LEAF

Bitter leaf is bitter to the taste when fresh. But it is tasty when cooked as a vegetable in your stew. It is very good for your health. It fights against diabetes, fights against bad vision, fights against tuberculoses and rheumatism. Bitter leaf is a good vegetable.

BLUEBERRIES

Blueberries are fruits of knowledge. Eating Blueberries freshens your memory and makes your eyes clear. Blueberries will give you low cholesterol and Fights cancer. It is one of the best fruits you may find to eat.

BREAD

Matthew_14:_17&19
¹⁷And they say unto him, we have here but five loaves, and two fishes. ¹⁹And he commanded the multitude to sit down on the grass, and took the five loaves, and the two fishes, and looking up to heaven, he blessed, and brake, and gave the loaves to his disciples, and the disciples to the multitude.

These verses will make you realize that bread is one of the best foods so much that Jesus recognized it. He blessed it and he fed the multitude with it. Bread is very good for your health. Especially the brown bread which helps maintains a healthy weight and strong bone. (*Read_2_Sam_9vs_10).*

BROCCOLI

Broccoli is a special vegetable that helps fight cancer, strengthens your bones, and give you a clear vision. It also protects you from heart diseases and lowers your blood pressure. Cooking it with rice, or like vegetable is delicious.

CABBAGE

There are two kinds of cabbage (green & purple) and they both perform the same function in your health. (1) Protect your heart (2) refresh your kidney (3) fight against cancer (4) it helps your digestive system and lower your blood sugar. You can eat it in any way you want. Eat it fresh with rice. You can produce juice out of it. All is well.

CASSAVA

There are two different types of Cassavas:
You can get good starch from Cassavas. Cassava is a good food if you can follow the instructions. African people make (Garri) from Cassava, and they make (Eba) from (Garri). Ghanaians make different kind of food from cassava. Also Trinidad and Jamaicans have different ways of eating cassava. It is an international food. But follow the instruction about cooking, or frying, or pounding before you eat it. It is very delicious. It will *refresh your brain, clear your eyes, settle your stomach, smoothens your blood flow and it also makes your skin fresh*. Warning: eating fresh cassava without cooking is dangerous.

CASSAVA LEAVES

Cassava leaf is also known as vegetable; a lot of people don't know that after cooking, it's tasty, eat it with any food you will realize that it is good for your heart. It will refresh your brain; clear your eyes settle your stomach smoothen your blood flow and it will also make your skin fresh. Warning: eating fresh cassava leaves without cooking is dangerous.

CASHEW

The water from fresh Cashew and the juice are very good to clean your heart. It will help your kidney. It is also useful for diabetic patients. Warning: The water from the fresh cashew's nut is very dangerous for your skin but roosted cashew's nuts give you a lot of iron and make your bone strong.

CANTALOUPE

Eating Cantaloupe once or twice a week helps saves your eyesight, boosts your immune system, controls your blood pressure and lowers cholesterol.

CARROTS

Cooking carrot with your food regularly protects you from heart attacks, settles your stomach, destroys cancer, gives you a better vision and it helps you loss weight. Eating fresh carrot gives you energy and it is good for all pregnant women.

CAULIFLOWER

Cauliflower does the work as a carrot, but it has a specific protection from cancer. It protects you from Prostate and Breast Cancer. It gives you strong bone and also protect you from heart disease. By boiling cauliflower before eating gives you all the nutrition.

CHERRIES

Cherries are supernatural fruits. It is very good for those that have skin disease. It filters your blood and protects your heart. It is tasty if you eat fresh cherries and you can make it into juice. Eating dinner with cherry juice will give you more vitamins and will quickly digest your food. Cherries help your low blood and fights against cancer.

CHESTNUTS

Chestnuts fight against high cholesterol. It provides more iron for you and makes your bones strong. Roast or cook it very well before you eat it.

COCOYAM

There are different types of Cocoyam and different ways to eat it. It is a good food. But follow the instructions before cooking, frying, or pounding. It is very delicious. It will settle your stomach, smoothen your blood running. Warning: eating fresh cocoyam without cooking is dangerous

COCONUT

Coconut water cleans your stomach, and kidney. Eating fresh inner coconut is good for Refreshment because it's tasty. We can get coconut rice, oil, juice and a lot of things from coconut

COCOA

Cocoa is a fruit that is used to produce Bon Vita, chocolate, cake and cookies using its seed. Eating all cocoa products will give you energy and strong bones. Cocoa seed's water is very good for fighting against Kidney problems and you can use a little fresh cocoa seeds to prepare stews like okra. This is also good for heart problem; Cocoa is one of the pure fruits from above.

COFFEE FRUIT

These are the coffee fruit that provide coffee tea. The new coffee leave is stronger than coffee tea. We all know the advantages and disadvantages of coffee. Coffee is a good tea, but too much of it is not good for your health. Balance yourself on coffee in your breakfast time will help you fight against prostate cancer. Coffee helps clot blood disease. But if you are hypertensive, stay away from coffee.

CORN

Corn is a very healthy fruit. It helps your memory, makes your blood flow very easily. Corns are good for your skin. There are many ways that you can eat corn. Cooking it, peeling it and mixing it with beans and

putting it in the oven. Corn helps your vision. Corn gives you strength and protein and African people use corn to make pap (EKO). Genesis 43vs 2 ²And it came to pass, when they had eaten up the corn which they had brought out of Egypt, their father said unto them, Go again, buy us a little food.

CRAB

Genesis 1 vs. 30
³⁰And to every beast of the earth, and to every fowl of the air, and to every thing that creepeth upon the earth, wherein there is life, I have given every green herb for meat: and it was so.

God has blessed everything he created to be a meal for us and everything that God created is Holy. So do not be among of the people that hate crabs. Crab gives protein, freshen your brain and makes your skin fresh. When you see Chinese people, you will realize the advantage of seafood in their skin and in their health. By eating crabs once in a while, it will give you a long sight and you will feel healthy.

CUCUMBER

Numbers 11:5
We remember the fish, which we did eat in Egypt freely; the cucumbers, and the melons, and the leeks, and the onions, and the garlic:

Eating Cucumber at least three times every week can make you lose weight, lowers your cholesterol and controls your blood pressure. It is delicious if you mix it together with what the Bible verse told us in Numbers 11 vs. 5 in your lunch or dinner. It will give you a nice sleep.

EGGS

Eggs gives protein and it makes your bones strong, also provides more blood. Egg is good for every one especially pregnant women. Eat two eggs every week will give you more blood.

FIGS

Matthew_21:19
And when he saw a fig tree in the way, he came to it, and found nothing thereon, but leaves only, and said unto it, Let no fruit grow on thee henceforward for ever. And presently the fig tree withered away.

Figs are very good for your <u>weight loss, protect you against stroke, lower your high cholesterol and control your blood pressure</u>. Roasting the nuts inside figs before eating will give you more iron. Figs are very important fruits. The bible verse above explains that the fig tree is the only tree that Jesus came to in the bible. If this tree wasn't important, Jesus wouldn't have visited it for fruit, and as we all know anything that Jesus like is good for your health.

FISH

Matthew_15:34—And Jesus saith unto them, How many loaves have ye? And they said, Seven, and a few little fishes.

Matthew_15:36—And he took the seven loaves and the fishes, and gave thanks, and brake them, and gave to his disciples, and the disciples to the multitude.

You can imagine how important, delicious and the recommendation giving to fish through Jesus Christ. We don't need to waste too much of our time before you know the help that fish does in your health. It gives protein, refreshes your brain, bright vision and strong bone. It is a balance diet if you can follow the instruction written in the book of Numbers 11 vs. 5

Numbers 11:5
We remember the fish, which we did eat in Egypt freely; the cucumbers, and the melons, and the leeks, and the onions, and the garlic:

FLAX

Flax fruit is very scarce and difficult to find, but it is fruit that maintains your brains and protects your blood against diseases. Cooking it and eating it like peanut is tasty and makes you healthy.

GARLIC

Numbers 11:5
We remember the fish, which we did eat in Egypt freely; the cucumbers, and the melons, and the leeks, and the onions, and the garlic:

Cooking garlic with your food can make you lose weight, lowers your cholesterol and controls your blood pressure. It is delicious if you mix it together with what the Bible verse told us in Numbers 11 vs. 5 in your lunch or dinner. It will also help your heart problem.

GINGER

Ginger is a natural fruit, cleans your veins, stomach, heart, kidney and liver. Protects you from high cholesterol and fights against fever and typhoid. Cook it in a pot and drink the water like tea, you will enjoy it.

GUAVA

Guava juice and the fruit are natural and good for your health. Especially the green fruit guava cleans your heart, liver and kidney. The yellow fruit guava provides you more blood. Guava is a nice fruit. The ripe yellow fruit guava is tasty, but the green fruit is sour but makes you healthy.

GRAPEFRUIT & GRAPES

There are different types of Grapes but they do the same work in your health, both the small ones and the big ones. Grape's water protect you from cancer, fight against over large Adam's apple, battles elephantiasis and it saves your eyesight. It fights against germs from Hepatitis and kidney problem. Grapes clean the liver of those that are suffering from typhoid. Grapes promote weight loss and helps stops strokes. All diabetic patients should keep away from grapes.

KIWI

Kiwi fruit is very scarce and difficult to find, but it is fruit that maintains your liver and protects your kidney and cleans your blood. Eating it after food will make you healthy.

LEMONS & LIMES

Lemon and Limes are both the same and they are useful for a lot of things. Drinking both their water and juice once in a week will save your liver against Hepatitis A, B and C. It also protects your kidney. Notice, constant boils is sign of Kidney problem or Cancer. It protects you from oversized Adam's apple. Mixing limes or lemon's water to clean your pot will protect you from diseases.

LETTUCE

Lettuce is a very good vegetable. It will make you healthy. Eat fresh lettuce with fresh tomatoes, cucumber, orange fruits and pineapple after food; it will give you a nice sleep and balance diet. It also helps people's memory and makes your skin fresh. It makes you strong and settles your stomach.

MANGOES

Yellow mangoes works like tonic in your blood and also flushes your stomach. The green mangoes fights against typhoid, cancer, overlarge Adams apples, elephantiasis, and protects you from diseases. We make juice, pies, cakes and roasted nut through mangoes. All do the same work in your health, but too much of it is not good.

MUSHROOM

Mushrooms control your blood pressure, settle your stomach, give you more blood and protect you against heart attack. You will enjoy mushrooms by cooking it with your stew and it lowers your cholesterol.

OATS

Do you have high cholesterol, cancer or are you over weight? Wheat bran should be your favourite breakfast. It will help you from all these problems. It can also help your digestive system. It is good with warm water and little low-fat milk. It also helps diabetic patients.

OKRA

Romans_14_vs._1-4_and_6
¹Him that is weak in the faith receive ye, but not doubtful disputations. ²For one believeth that he may eat all things: another, who is weak, eateth herbs. ³Let not him that eateth; despise him that eateth not and let not him that eateth not judge him that eateth: for God has received him.

Okra is a vegetable. You don't need to hate it because it is slimy. Eating Okra stew will give you high Vitamins A, and C, as well as protein and iron. Cook it very well before eating.

ONIONS

Numbers_11:5
We remember the fish, which we did eat in Egypt freely; the cucumbers, and the melons, and the leeks, and the onions, and the garlic:

Cooking onion with any food helps weight loss, lowers cholesterol and controls blood pressure. It is delicious if mixed with what the Bible reminds us in Numbers 11^{vs}5 at lunch or dinner. It will give you a nice sleep.

ORANGES & TANGERINE

Orange is good for you after food. It will help digest your food quickly and settle your stomach. Oranges help those that have hard congestion. It will purge you after eating about 3 inner orange fruit a day. Some causes of headache come from hard congestion. Hard congestion means not able to go to toilet regularly. This might cause headache. Orange will solve headaches caused by hard congestion. Tangerine cleans your heart and fight against lung cancer. You can make juice from orange and tangerine and the natural juice does the same work also with the fruit.

PALM FRUIT

We produce Palm oil from palm fruit; palm fruit comes from palm tree. Prepare your stew with little palm oil, not too much, all the time. Too much oil can cause high cholesterol in cold countries. But cooking little palm oil with your stew makes you healthy or use the raw palm oil to eat plantain, yam or potato. It will help your heart and kill germs that can cause disease in your blood, and it makes your skin fresh. We make a lot of things from palm kennel, but palm oil is good oil.

PAWPAW

Both yellow and green pawpaw protects you against heart attack. Green pawpaw fights against typhoid and cancer. Pawpaw is useful for a lot of things in your health. For example, scientists discover HIV through the blood of gorillas and imagine how it doesn't harm them because of the green leaves and fruit they eat in the forest. So every fruits that animals like bring health to the life human beings. So pawpaw is one the best fruit in the forest. Eat pawpaw the way you like it at least twice in a month, especially the green ones, it will make you healthy.

PEACHES

Peaches cleanse your blood and help your blood flow smoothly. One peach after your exercise helps your heart and makes it beat normally. Peaches settle your stomach and make you feel comfortable.

PEAR

Pears are healthy fruits. It's good to eat some pears after lunch. You will be energized all day. Pears make your blood flow smoothly and fight against Hepatitis and cough.

PEANUTS

Do you need more iron in your blood? If yes peanuts are good for you. But it's not good for those that have high blood pressure. Eating peanuts once in a week will help your bones to be strong. We get oil, butter and cookies in peanuts. Peanuts fights against germs in your blood. Peanuts are high-level sources of protein. Groundnut is known as peanut. It is found all over the world. Do not eat too much peanut. And if you are allergic to peanut, do not eat any type.

PEPPERS (RED, YELLOW, GREEN, ORANGE & CHILI)

There are different types of pepper with different colours. Pepper produces more blood for humans and it cures a lot of virus that could cause diseases through flies or mosquito. Good luck to any one that likes to eat hot pepper. It fights against diseases that can affect us through the animals that we eat such as goat, cow, pork, chicken and bird. That is not the end, hot pepper protect you against cancer. Hot pepper is enemy of terrible and constant headaches. It helps sore throat and chase away cold instantly. Eating fresh pepper with fruit after lunch or after exercise gives you a smooth skin and makes you look younger.

PINEAPPLE

Pineapple fights against skin sickness. Pineapple juice cleans your heart, kidney, liver and fights against cancer. Mix pineapple with vegetable and eat it after food will make you healthy. Some people cook pineapple with stew. Finally, pineapple is a good supernatural fruit and it strengthens your bones.

PLANTAIN

Plantain makes you strong. It refreshes your brain. One plantain covers four tablets of pain killers. Green plantains have high levels of iron. "It can either be cooked or roasted". It fights against diabetes. Eating, cooking, or roasting plantain will also help your bones. You can make plantain powder through plantain, and fried yellow plantain makes your body fresh, eating fresh yellow plantain without frying fights against coughs. We can also make cake through yellow plantain. Plantain is useful for your health and makes you healthy.

PRUNES

There are many different types of prunes. But the green ones and the red ones are the most popular. Prunes are very delicious fruits. Prunes protect you against heart disease. Eating prunes will lower your cholesterol and settles your stomach.

POMEGRANATE

It is tasty, provides you more blood and cleans your vein, high in vitamin A and C. It gives you more proteins and energy. Also strengthen your bones. Too much of it can make you fat. It is a good fruit in your health. Diabetic people should beware of it. It is sugary.

RICE

Rice is one of the most famous foods all over the world. Rice has a lot of starch; it is a common and favourite food for a lot of people. It makes you healthy and fights against <u>obesity</u> in your blood by digesting quickly. Cooking beans and corn with some vegetables with your rice gives you a <u>balance diet.</u>

SHRIMPS

Genesis 1 vs. 30
³⁰And to every beast of the earth, and to every fowl of the air, and to every thing that creepeth upon the earth, wherein there is life, I have given every green herb for meat: and it was so.

God has blessed everything he created to be a meal for us and everything that God created is Holy. So, do not be among of the people that dislike shrimps. Shrimps give <u>protein</u>, freshens the brain and make your <u>skin fresh</u>. When you see Chinese people, you will realize the advantage of seafood in their skin and in their health. By eating shrimps once in a while it will give you a <u>long sight</u> and you will feel healthy. You can eat fresh shrimps with vegetables and you can cook it with stew.

SOUR SOP

The pulp of this fruit is creamy and may be eaten as it is, used for ice cream or for juice. The fruit is large, can weigh as much as six pounds and take between 20 and 25 weeks to reach maturity. The tree of this fruit may reach a height of about thirty feet.

Sour sops protect the gums of your teeth and makes your teeth strong; It helps your brain a lot and fights germs in your blood. It washes away any dirt in your organs and clear your eyesight. Sour sops are very good.

STRAWBERRIES

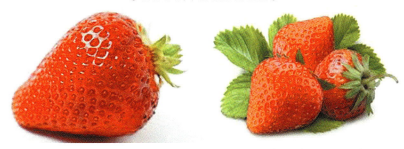

Strawberries flush your stomach, cleanse your kidney, protect you from heart attack and protect your blood from Hepatitis. Strawberry juice is also good and does the works as well as the cake. They are all good for your health.

SNAIL

GENESIS_1_VS_30_&_31
30And to every beast of the earth, and to every fowl of the air, and to every thing that creepeth upon the earth, wherein there is life, I have given every green herb for meat: and it was so. 31And God saw

every thing that he had made, and, behold, it was very good. And the evening and the morning were the sixth day.

All what God has created, the scripture tells us in the book of Genesis 1 verse 31 that it was very good but a lot of people dislike snail because it crawls. It is only things that are used for sacrifice to idols that are forbidden for a child of God to eat. Meanwhile, cooking snail in your stew or boil it for lunch will help your brain and clean your eyes. It is also good for your skin because it will make it fresh.

SWEET POTATOES

Sweet potato is sweet and delicious, after cooking. Eat it regularly it will clean your eyesight, strengthen your bones and make your blood run smoothly. It will make you healthy.

SUGAR CANE

Sugar cane has a supernatural sugar, but it is not good for diabetic people. We produce sugar through sugar cane. Sugar cane is good for people with low blood sugar. We make some juice through sugar cane. Sugar cane is sweet and tasty.

SPINACH

Spinach vegetables are supernatural from God. If you are suffering from low blood pressure, heart disease, kidney problems or constipation, this is your right vegetable. Eat it constantly with little salt, you can eat fresh spinach with your rice or cook it with stew, it is very tasty and you will be healthy.

TOMATOES

We don't need to explain to you before you know the importance of tomatoes in your health, especially fresh tomatoes. It fights against heart disease and kidney problems. If you suffer from Hepatitis also called Typhoid in Africa, tomatoes will protect your liver. It helps your digestive system and gives you a delicious taste in your food.

WALNUTS

Walnuts gives you iron, it lowers your cholesterol, fight against heart disease and cancer. Walnuts are just like refreshment. But some people produce oil, cake, cookies and some other things from it. Anything you see that is produced from it is good for you if you are suffering from any of the above diseases.

WATER

Revelation 22:2
In the midst of the street of it, and on either side of the river, was there the tree of life, which bare twelve manners of fruits, and yielded her fruit every month: and the leaves of the tree were for the healing of the nations.

This verse tells us the important of water that you must recognise it and what it means to your life. Clean water cure diseases. Drinking a lot of clean water lowers your blood pressure. Drink up to six cups of clean water every day helps your liver and your kidney and it also smoothens your skin.

WATERMELON

Numbers 11:5
We remember the fish, which we did eat in Egypt freely; the cucumbers, and the melons, and the leeks, and the onions, and the garlic:

Eating Watermelon can make you lose weight, lowers your cholesterol and controls your blood pressure. It is delicious if you mix it together with what the Bible verse told us in Numbers 11 vs. 5 with your lunch or dinner. It will give you a nice sleep.

WHEAT GERM

Do you have high cholesterol or are you over weight? Wheat germ should be your favourite breakfast. It will help you from all these problems. It can also help your digestive system. It is good with warm water and little low-fat milk.

WHEAT BRAN

Do you have high **cholesterol** or are you **over weight?** Wheat bran should be your favourite breakfast. It will help you from all these problems. It can also help your **digestive system.** It is good with warm water and little low-fat milk.

YAM

Yam is a strong and solid food. It has a lot of starch. Yam is good for you if you lack starch in your diet. You can make it into pounded yam, fried, boil, roosted or yam porridge. All are good for your health.

The Word of Appreciation

I thank God Almighty for the success of this book. Big thanks to everyone; my family and members of our Churches **ISREALITES CHURCH OF CHRIST W/W & JESUS MINISRY OF ISREALITE INC.** for their support on my heart desires, may the Lord God, Jesus Christ be with you all (Amen).

I use this opportunity to thank all my readers, I pray for the rain of mercy and blessing of God for you all (Amen).

I would also like to ask all Christians to pray for me, for my success to the kingdom of God. May God in his infinite mercy bless you all (Amen).

OTHER BOOKS BY REV JOHN P. OLAREWAJU

Interpretation of Dreams and Amazing Power of Prayers
Marriage Crises and Resolutions
Do the Right Thing you will be Saved
Star Charger

YOU CAN ALSO LOOK FORWARD TO MY NEW BOOKS

Do not lose hope! With daily psalms and prayer
The book of wisdom
101 PROBLEMS AND THE SOLUTIONS jonah's Journey
The success of your children
400 dreams, interpretation and solutions
The book of holy Mary
Ananiahs and Safiah

Edwards Brothers, Inc.
Thorofare, NJ USA
January 20, 2012